DIVORCE & REMARRY

IS MAN'S ALTERNATIVE, NOT GOD'S PLAN

"He said to them, "Moses, because of the hardness of your hearts, permitted you to divorce your wives, but from the beginning it was not so"

(Matthew19:8 NKJV).

TONY O AKPATI

Divorce & Remarry (is man's alternative, not God's plan) The First Edition 2016
Copyright @ 2016 Anthony O. Akpati

ISBN 978-0-9913641-1-4

Unless otherwise noted, all scripture is from the King James Version of the Bible © 1982 by Thomas Nelson, Inc. Used by permission. Scripture quotations marked NKJV are from the New King James Version of the Bible.

Cover Design and Layout by

MYPRO DESIGN – 214 228-4278

The King's House Publications
The King's House Ministries. Plano Texas
Email: info@thekingshouselive.org,
Email: toniakpati@yahoo.com ,
toniakpati@gmail.com, Website:
www.thekingshouselive.org

DEDICATION

To the glory of the Lord, I am dedicating this book to all those going through problems in their marriages and are still holding on to the promises of God. I make a commitment to be praying for you that God will calm every storm rocking the boat of your marriage and grant you peace in Jesus name.

ACKNOWLEDGEMENT

But there is a spirit in man: and the inspiration of the Almighty giveth them understanding (Job 32:8).

I give God all the glory for giving me the inspiration to write this book. I want to say thank you to my wife Paulina, my children Israel, Daniel and Precious. As always, you have been there for me. Thank you for your love, and support. I want you to know that you are a vital and indispensable part of this project. I love you all.

I want to say special thanks to all those who have been supporting us in the work of the ministry through their fellowship, giving and prayers.

I also want to say special thanks to Mrs. Rose Obilor who has been a mother to me, for her motherly counsel and encouragement. We call her mummy Rose. Also, I want to say thank you to Pastor and Mrs. Yomi Osinaike, Pastor and Mrs. Isaac Idemudia, Pastor and Mrs. Niyi Obamehinti, Pastor and Mrs. James Olaleye, and

Pastor and Mrs. Steve Amuda, Pastor Karen Muigai, all of Winners Chapel International Dallas and the entire ministerial team for the opportunity given me to serve in the ministry, for their love, prayers and encouragement. Dr. and Mrs. Emmanuel Fasanya, you have been a great blessing to me and my family. Words are not enough to convey how much we cherish you and your family. Doc, you are not just a brother you are a friend. I always see you as my big brother. Thank you for your labour of love. I really appreciate you.

My appreciation also goes to Mike Gill, my co-worker, who did the first correction in this book, my children, Israel, Daniel, and Precious who cross-checked the Bible references, Pastor Wales Goriola who did the layout and formatting, and Brother Gbenga Olowo who completed the formatting and designed the cover. Our Heavenly Father who sees in secret will reward you openly for all that you do for his kingdom's sake in Jesus name.

FOREWORD

On behalf of all who earnestly seek to live the joy and completeness given us the day we stood before God in marriage and said "I do", "This Book" is intended to support and enlighten!! Every chapter is empowered for you by God's word and personal experience. Jesus promised in John 8:31-32 "Then said Jesus to those Jews which believed on him, If ye continue in my word, then are ye my disciples indeed; And ye shall know the truth, and the truth shall make you free". Unfortunately, we are living in a culture today that does not subscribe or give support to "abiding or knowing God's word for our marriages"! Our society's norm seems to advocate the attitude that, "If it feels good, do it" in the subject of "marriage & divorce"! Most especially we are "not free" living outside of God's word (John 8:32), as the truth in Tony's writing reveals deep insights, enlightening our understanding of God's best, to indeed, be "set free" (guiltless, peace, righteousness)! Tony's, experience as Pastor, husband, teacher, "understanding counselor" clergyman and writer provides astute clarity and simplicity in what otherwise has been very confusing in the past. The number one concern in our world today should be, "The Family"! "The family", is America's and the world's first primary institution! All other institutions depend upon "The Family"! America's and the world's institutions, financial educational, religious, medical, political etc. all depend on families and strong marriages! Tony's concise understanding on commitment, steps toward healing, conflict resolution and facing realistic "How to guidance" is an inclusive approach to marriage, along with our unique personhood is vital for every marriage and family.

If marriage and family is weak or broken, America and the world will be weak and broken!! I was most impressed with the beginning five chapters as Tony provided steps on the much needed and much neglected issue on "How-to-make-wise-choices" in the secular world that ignores this subject! We all need to "grow in emotional and spiritual maturity, which Tony reinforces with valuable examples and scenarios. This is a necessary "HOW TO" book for devastating times, living in a secular environment, struggling to keep marriage and family living under God's blessing "knowing the truth that sets us free". You will not be able to put this Book down. It guides, exposes, gives insight, knowledge, understanding and hope in facing marriage, at all its stages. This should be a "Manual" for all engaged couples, newlyweds, pre-divorce courts and church counselors!

Bunny Kopinski

"Blessed wife", married 50 years, now widowed, Mother of 5 adult children and 13 grandchildren, A leader of Women's Bible study Groups since 1975 and Substance abuse counselor from 1991 to 1999 (CADAC stf.) Tech. Recruiter/counselor

TABLE OF CONTENTS

INTRODUCTION

A MESSAGE FOR YOU

We live in a fallen world, a world that has moved out of its original course and is on an entirely different one (Psalm 82:5). The ways of the world is in direct opposition to the ways of the Lord. *For my thoughts are not your thoughts, neither are your ways my ways, says the Lord* (Isaiah 55:8). A lot of things that are normal from the world's point of view are abnormal in God's kingdom. The Lord enjoined his children to come out of this world's way of thinking and their way of living.

Wherefore come out from among them, and be ye separate, saith the Lord, and touch not the unclean thing; and I will receive you (2 Corinthians 6:17)

Jesus speaking to the Father about his disciples said; *"They are not of the world, even as I am not of the world* (John 17:16).

In other words, even though we live in this world we should not live according to the precepts of the world's system.

And be not conformed to this world: but be ye transformed by the renewing of your mind, that ye may prove what is that good, and acceptable, and perfect, will of God (Romans 12:2).

One of the foremost marks of a child of God is living in obedience to the word of God. When anyone is living a life inconsistent with the word of God and claims to be a child of God, obviously something is wrong with the person. Merely declaring that I am a citizen of the United State of America does not make me one. I should be able to validate my claims by showing the proof of my citizenship. Hear what Jesus said:

Then said Jesus to those Jews which believed on him, If ye continue in my word, then are ye my disciples indeed (John 8:31).

When children of God divorce and remarry contrary to God's word, it brings pollution in the church and in the land and it depletes the power of God in the church. If you read through the word of God you will discover that there is no aspect of our lives as humans, even as children of God, that is not addressed in the scriptures. The condition for divorce is not left out. God did not leave us in the dark to figure out what to do in such situations. Neither did he delegate the divorce attorneys to decide what to do. It is well spelt out in the word of God. There are also conditions to remarry in the bible, not what we have today in the church. Divorce and re-marry as we have today is man's alternative, it is not God's plan.

For my people have committed two evils; they have forsaken me the fountain of living waters, and hewed them out cisterns, broken cisterns, that can hold no water. (Jeremiah 2:13)

The Spirit of God impressed it upon my heart to write this book, to address this issue which the church has been living with as though it is the will of God. The church is blending with the culture. Statistics has it that the rate of divorce in the church is the same with those outside the church. Jesus said: *You are the salt of the earth* – Matthew 5:13. It appears the salt is gradually

3

losing its taste. The church is full of adulterers and adulteresses. Hear what Jesus said:

And I say unto you, whosoever shall put away his wife, except it be for fornication, and shall marry another, committeth adultery: and whoso marrieth her which is put away doth commit adultery (Matthew 19:9).

There is no ambiguity in the above statement that the Lord Jesus made. It does not need any special interpretation. It is self explanatory. To do anything contrary to the word of God is complete disobedience. You can justify your actions; men can give you their approval, including men of God. Neither does that make it right before God nor does it mean that God approved of it. I have heard people use the term," irreconcilable differences". There is nothing like that in the bible. The bible calls that the hardness of heart; a heart that is so adamant that it rejects God's word concerning the issue. We are called obedient children in the book of first Peter chapter one in verse fourteen. We are not to make our own rules but we are to follow the rules of God. One of the major problems that we have as humans is the problem of selfishness. Humans are so self-centered that they want everything to revolve around them. It is either his way or her way or no other way. Just as the earth revolves around the sun, everything about us as children of God should revolve around the Son of God, Jesus, who is the Sun of righteousness (Malachi 4:2).

Paul the apostle re-echoed the statements of Jesus when he said:

And unto the married I command, yet not I, but the Lord, Let not the wife depart from her husband: But and if she depart, let her remain unmarried or be reconciled to her husband: and let not the husband put away his wife (1 Corinthians 7: 10-11).

The Pharisees also came unto him, tempting him, and saying unto him, Is it lawful for a man to put away his wife for every cause? And he answered and said unto them, Have ye not read, that he which made them at the beginning made them male and female, And said, For this cause shall a man leave father and mother, and shall cleave to his wife: and they twain shall be one flesh? Wherefore they are no more twain, but one flesh.

What therefore God hath joined together, let not man put asunder. They say unto him, why did Moses then command to give a writing of divorcement, and to put her away? He saith unto them, Moses because of the hardness of your hearts suffered you to put away your wives: but from the beginning it was not so (Matthew 19:3-8).

Be careful of whom you receive counsel from, and the kind of counsel you receive.

I have seen also in the prophets of Jerusalem an horrible thing: they commit adultery, and walk in lies: they strengthen also the hands of evildoers, that none doth return from his wickedness; they are all of them unto me as Sodom, and the inhabitants thereof as Gomorrah (Jeremiah 23:14).

Many minister of the gospel sugar-coat the word of God, leaving God's people with a watered-down version of the word. They deceive God's people and will not tell them the whole truth because they don't want to lose them as members. And some of them preach their own version of the gospel, the "all inclusive" gospel, a message that do not rebuke sin or call for repentance from sin. This they do so that the offerings and tithes will not diminish. Do not mistake their devotion for the truth. One can be devoted to a wrong course and not know it. There are some men of God that do not hear from God, so they tell you what they think. The duty of the pastor is to uphold the word of God. He is a messenger of God and as such he is not there to give his opinion on what God says about any issue. He is called to enforce the word of God by preaching the undiluted, unadulterated and non compromising gospel of Jesus Christ. The gospel of Christ is an everlasting gospel. It neither changes with time nor does it fluctuates with any dispensation. God is looking for people that will do his will. The reason why God removed Saul from being the king of Israel and replaced him with David was because he stopped following God's command. Instead he chose to please the people at the expense of God's instructions. (1 Samuel 13:13-14). You can't follow a casual approach if you truly want to please God. No, you can't be lukewarm. It takes diligence to live in obedience to God. You must pay careful attention to what you do or say. Paul said in the book of Galatians chapter one in verse ten:

For do I now persuade men, or God? or do I seek to please men? for if I yet pleased men, I should not be the servant of Christ.

Yet, there are some so called men of God that are not of God. They are messengers of the devil, carrying on the devil's mission of deception.

For such people are false apostles, deceitful workers, masquerading as apostles of Christ. And no wonder, for Satan himself masquerades as an angel of light. It is not surprising, then, if his servants also masquerade as servants of righteousness. Their end will be what their actions deserve. (2 Corinthians 11:13-15)

With all sense of humility, America is not the standard for the church of Jesus Christ. The Bible, which is the living word of God, is the standard. That's why the bible says in the book of Hebrews chapter twelve in verse two:

Looking unto Jesus the author and finisher of our faith; who for the joy that was set before him endured the cross, despising the shame, and is set down at the right hand of the throne of God.

Jesus is the word of God. Don't look unto any culture. I plead with you in the name of Jesus; don't give up on your marriage. Do not throw in the towel.Running away has never been a solution to crisis in marriage, getting a new spouse is not a solution either. Take that issue to God in prayer. God still answers prayers don't let anyone deceive you. The essence of this message is not to condemn anyone but for us to consider our ways and make things right with God. What will it profit a man if he gets a new wife and lose his own soul (paraphrasing Mark 8:36). You don't need a new wife; you need a new life in Christ Jesus. Likewise the woman, you don't need a new man but a new life in Christ Jesus.

Therefore if any man be in Christ, he is a new creature: old things are passed away; behold all things are become new (2 Corinthians 5:17).

Paul said, "*Be ye transformed by the renewing of your mind*" - Romans 12:2.God wants a people with contrite heart, not concrete heart, people that will humble themselves at his word. The reason why the devil has fought so much to discredit the bible and is still fighting is to remove any moral judgment for people's action, whether those actions are good or bad. I am not writing from the moon, I live in the midst of this crooked and perverse generation, the same world you live in. I have been married for just fourteen years now. We have weathered through many turbulent storms and are still weathering, but we chose to stand by God's word. Divorce is not an option. Beware of anyone that tells you that they never had any issue in their marriage. Marital crisis is not a strange phenomenon. Hear what the bible says in the book of second Peter chapter four in verse twelve:

Beloved, think it not strange concerning the fiery trial which is to try you, as though some strange thing happened unto you

God did not promise any one a problem-free life but he gave us the assurance that we will overcome them. Jesus said "*In the world ye shall have tribulation: but be of good cheer; I have overcome the world* (John 16:33). The prophet Isaiah puts it this way; *when thou passest through the waters, I will be with thee; and through the rivers, they shall not overflow thee: when thou walkest through the fire, thou shalt not be burned; neither shall the flame kindle upon thee* (Isaiah 43:2).

I remember an analogy one of my teachers gave to us in church while speaking about marriage. He said it is like when someone wants to make a smoothie, you add different kinds of fruit into the blender. At the beginning the mixing will be rough and noisy but after sometime the mixing becomes smooth and noiseless because the fruits have blended well together. The result is a delicious smoothie for you to enjoy. This made a lot of sense to me. There are people you might know; maybe your parents that stayed in their marriage for, thirty, forty, fifty and even more years and yet have no plans of getting out. It doesn't mean that it has been a bed of roses. It does not mean that they never had any misunderstanding, quarrel, argument, or problem in their marriage. They chose to stand by God's word and their marriage vows against all odds.

Hear the words of Jesus,

"Therefore whosoever heareth these sayings of mine, and doeth them, I will liken him unto a wise man, which built his house upon a rock: And the rain descended, and the floods came, and the winds blew, and beat upon that house; and it fell not: for it was founded upon a rock. And every one that heareth these sayings of mine, and doeth them not, shall be likened unto a foolish man, which built his house upon the sand: And the rain descended, and the floods came, and the winds blew, and beat upon that house; and it fell: and great was the fall of it (Matthew 7:24-27).

The two houses experienced the same weather conditions, the rain, the floods the winds, but they came out with varying results, based on their attitude towards the word of God. As you can see, doing what the word of God commands does not stop trials from coming but it guarantees victory over any circumstance. Most problems that we have today, even as Christians, largely depends on the fact that we do not do what the word of God command us to do.

"But be ye doers of the word, and not hearers only, deceiving your own selves (James 1:22)".

It is my utmost desire and my prayer that through this book God will restore peace to homes, heal marriages, equip and empower the saints so as to live a godly life that will influence the rest of the world to the glory of his name, in Jesus name. Amen.

Jesus is Lord.

CHAPTER ONE

GOD IS THE AUTHOR OF
MARRIAGE

Marriage is not man's idea; it is God's idea. There is no gainsaying of the fact that there is absolute truth irrespective of people's views and opinions. Some things that are absurd and should be abhorred are now considered fashionable. It may interest you to know that of all God's creation, it is only humans that undermine the authority of God and his word. Men have subjugated the word of God as if it is no more relevant, to the detriment of their life. "*There is no wisdom nor understanding nor counsel against the Lord*" (Proverbs 21:30). There is no level of scientific and technological advancement that can place man above God. No doubt, God gave man certain inalienable rights but that does not place man in the position of God. Anyone, any nation that dares to change the law of God will only attracts the wrath of God. The government can decide to change the speed limit on any particular highway, which will not be an issue with God. This is because it is an administrative duty of the government to make such regulations. This is not the same with moral laws. Moral laws are from God and it is the duty of the civil government to enforce it. They do not have the right to change God's law. God did not give anyone the right to change his word, not even the divorce attorney has the right to provide for divorce.

Marriage is not just a contract; it is much more than that. It is a covenant enacted by God and sealed by blood, and as such, it is irrevocable. A lot of people have this idea that truth is subjective. Hear this; truth is absolute, and the word of God is truth. It is choice that is subjective not truth.

Sanctify them through thy truth: thy word is truth (John 17:17).

The views, opinions, and personal beliefs and feelings, which are individual choices, cannot take the place of the truth. The fact that God gave us the right to choose does not eliminate the truth of God's word. Choice is very good if we make the right ones. We must choose to follow God's instruction if we desire to get the best he has for us. The place of choice is very important in every aspect of our lives, including our marriages. I will like to take an excerpt from my first book, with a little modification, to emphasize the place of choice. I have come to realize that a lot of people do not understand the difference between their choice and what is right. A lot of people are in bondage today because of the choices they made.

A MATTER OF CHOICE

"I call heaven and earth as witnesses today against you, that I have set before you life and death, blessing and cursing; therefore choose life, that both you and your descendants may live." (Deuteronomy 30:19)

One of the greatest gifts that God ever gave to man is the gift of choice. This makes it man's responsibility to make decisions. Life is full of choices. Every day we are faced with alternatives to choose from. You can choose to pray, or watch the news, or surf the web, or watch movies. The Angels of God in their magnificent beauty, splendor and power do have the privilege of making choices. Unfortunately, a lot of people have abused this privilege, and turned again to blame God. The way anyone lives his or her life is a direct product of the choices he or she had made. In other words, the choices we make turn around to make us. The choices you make today control your present, and decide your future. Therefore, it becomes imperative for us to know what to choose in life. God made man a freewill moral agent. The will is a God-given force that is able to determine its choice and habits. We are humans, not robots; we have the will power to say no to any offer we don't want. Choice-making is inevitable in life; your decision not to make a choice is a choice in itself. God placed in every man what it takes to overcome trials and temptations but whether you overcome or not, is your choice.

THE RESPONSIBILITY OF CHOICE MAKING

God gave man the right to choose and even advised him to make the right choices. Choice-making is a personal non-transferable responsibility of man. You cannot hold anyone responsible for the choices you made. Whatever you decide to do is your business, but keep this in mind; there is an implication to every choice you make. You can choose to smoke, drink alcohol, do drugs, live immorally, or you can choose to live a decent and godly life. The law of seedtime and harvest is always in operation as long as this earth stands.

"While the earth remains, Seedtime and harvest, Cold and heat, Winter and summer, And day and night Shall not cease." (Genesis 8:22)

"Do not be deceived, God is not mocked; for whatever a man sows, that he will also reap." Galatians 6:7

You cannot make your choice and escape the consequence that goes with it. It comes as a complete package, the choice and its consequence. Anyone that chooses to smoke may end up with lung cancer if he or she refuses to change that habit. A sexually promiscuous person will end up with sexually transmitted disease if he or she continues with that habit. A pot smoker or a drug addict will end up losing his or her mind and end up losing everything he or she has labored for, and eventually end up in the streets or in jail. The choices you make have greater impact than you think. They do not only affect you, they affect your family and generations after you.

"For as by one man's disobedience many were made sinners, so also by one Man's obedience many will be made righteous." (Romans 5:19)

The generations after you do not have to do what you did to suffer the consequences of your choices, or enjoy the blessings thereof. The fact that they descended from you connects them to the consequences or the blessings. If children should continue in the same choice path as their parents, they only hasten the consequences or the blessing of those choices, as the case may be. When you make good and godly choices, you and generations after you will enjoy the blessings of God.

THE KEY TO MAKING CHOICES

The key to making a good choice amongst many alternatives is your ability to identify what is beneficial to you. The consequences of making wrong choices are grievous, and can be devastating. The pain you end up with by making a wrong choice by far outweighs the pleasure you derive from it.

"Choosing rather to suffer affliction with the people of God than to enjoy the passing pleasures of sin." (Hebrews 11:25)

There are so many things you might think are cool to do, but in the real sense of it, by doing those things you are actually destroying yourself and cutting your life short. I need to mention here that divorce is one of such things.

All things are lawful for me, but all things are not helpful. All things are lawful for me, but I will not be brought under the power of any." 1 Corinthians 6:12

The modern societies' cultures and traditions negate the word of God. They call evil good and call good evil. The scribes and Pharisees came to Jesus and said:

"Why do Your disciples transgress the tradition of the elders? For they do not wash their hands when they eat bread."He answered and said to them, "Why do you also transgress the commandment of God because of your tradition?" (Matthew 15:2-3)

The fact that something is lawful does not make it beneficial to you. To be skillful in choice making you must arm yourself with true and relevant information. The quality of choice one makes is dependent upon the information process available to him or her. When you have the wrong information you will definitely make the wrong choice. Unfortunately, many source their information about life only from the screen, the media, and the things they see and experience in the culture they live in. Information from these sources more often than not, is inconsistent and unreliable. This is because culture is dynamic and it changes with time. Culture has to do with geographical location, it is not universal. What is culturally acceptable in one country can be considered an abomination in another. At the other end of the spectrum of the information process are the proven truth, and the never changing word of God. It is universal and everlasting. It does not diminish or change with time. What God says in the United States of America is what he says in Europe. The same thing he says in Africa, Asia, and Australia. It cannot be influenced or altered by the Beijing conference, the Geneva Convention, the G8 summit, or the US Congress. You can bank on any information you obtain from this source. Your choice should be based on truth not on facts, emotions or feelings. Do you know that something can be a fact and yet not the truth? Any choice made based on the truth of God's word delivers its promises and secures your future. Any one that wants to escape the assaults of the satanic and evil demonic forces over his or her marriage must choose what God said about marriage above every belief, ideology or opinion of man that is contrary to God's word. Lord, grant me the grace to make the choice to always honor you in this body, as long as I live, that your name alone be glorified. Amen!

The author of marriage says that he hates divorce; the divorce attorney says it is ok to divorce. You are the one that makes the choice.

"For the Lord God of Israel says That He hates divorce, For it covers one's garment with violence," Says the Lord of hosts. "Therefore take heed to your spirit, That you do not deal treacherously" (Malachi 2:16 NKJV).

And if it seem evil unto you to serve the Lord, choose you this day whom ye will serve; whether the gods which your fathers served that were on the other side of the flood, or the gods of the Amorites, in whose land ye dwell: but as for me and my house, we will serve the Lord (Joshua 24:15)

Divorce is never a part of God's plan for anyone. The divorce attorneys do not have your interest at heart, all they want is to make an extra income through your problem. The choice is up to you. If only people can be patient and learn to forgive, things will work out at the end of the day. Do you know the reason why there is no curriculum on the subject of marriage? It is because marriage is not from man. Man's intellectual ability cannot handle the issue of marriage. Rely on God, the author of marriage for every of your life and marital issues. He will perfect everything that concerns you in Jesus precious name. Amen!

CHAPTER TWO

GOD HAS A PLAN
AND A **PURPOSE**

For I know the thoughts that I think toward you, saith the LORD, thoughts of peace, and not of evil, to give you an expected end (Jeremiah 29:11).

There is nothing God does that is without a purpose. As a matter of fact purpose is the number one factor that any manufacturer considers before initiating the manufacture of any product. The purpose of any product is not decided in the showroom after the product is made. When God brings a man and a woman into relationship in a marriage covenant it is for a purpose already established by him. We need to identify what this purpose is so as to apply ourselves to it, if we truly desire God's best for us. God has a general purpose for marriages and an individual purpose for each of our marriages. We need to find out what these purposes are. Until we successfully identify these purposes, we will be pursuing our selfish desires and comparing our marriages with those of others. Sex is not the purpose for marriage; it is one of the benefits of being married. As a matter of fact marriage was what God had in mind when he created sex. That is why sex outside marriage is wrong and it is a sin. This is not my opinion, it is God's law and that is his standard, and the standard has not changed. It has neither been reviewed nor has it been revoked, it stands throughout all ages regardless of peoples' views and opinions. Just as driving without a license is a violation of the law, so is sex outside marriage. It is a violation of the law of the Most High God. You need to read my first book "The Sex Conspiracy" to get more on the subject of sex. The purpose of God for marriage generally speaking is to establish the legacy of godliness. According to Malachi chapter two verse fifteen,

"*That he might seek a godly seed*".

Speaking about Abraham, God said:

For I know him, that he will command his children and his household after him, and they shall keep the way of the Lord, to do justice and judgment; that the Lord may bring upon Abraham that which he hath spoken of him (Genesis 18:19).

Secondly, God wants to use each marriage to demonstrate to the world his indescribable love. Humans are not perfect yet he loved us unconditionally. The bible has this to say about that,

"But God commendeth his love toward us, in that, while we were yet sinners, Christ died for us" (Romans 5:8).

If you are looking for a perfect man or a perfect woman to marry as a husband or wife you will not find one. We are all work in progress, at different levels striving towards the mark of Christ, nobody is there yet. I can guarantee you that. There is a flaw in the life of every human. This is not as a result of what we have done. It is a nature we inherited from birth (the sin nature), which was transmitted to us through Adam, as a result of the fall in Eden. This impacted every aspect of our being. It is only through salvation in Christ that the effect is minimized.

That I may know him, and the power of his resurrection, and the fellowship of his sufferings, being made conformable unto his death; if by any means I might attain unto the resurrection of the dead. Not as though I had already attained, either were already perfect: but I follow after, if that I may apprehend that for which also I am apprehended of Christ Jesus. Brethren, I count not myself to have apprehended: but this one thing I do, forgetting those things which are behind, and reaching forth unto those things which are before, I press toward the mark for the prize of the high calling of God in Christ Jesus (Philippians 3:10-14).

God wants us to demonstrate his love here on earth. Marriage is one of those opportunities to show the love of God. Many of God's children have the unrealistic expectation of how their spouses should be, what they should do and how they should act. I heard a heart breaking story of a woman that divorced her husband, leaving her four little children. According to the story, she left because her husband who is a medical doctor does not spend as much time as she desired, with her. God wants to demonstrate to the world that it is possible to genuinely love a person despite his or her shortcomings. God loves sinners but not their sins. Likewise we should be able to separate between a person and his or her shortcomings. When you successfully separate between the person and his shortcomings you will able love even as God wants us to love each other without any restriction or limitation. The truth is that when we answer "I do" during wedding ceremony we are saying "I do" to everything about the person. It is wrong to live with a man or a woman when you have not made this commitment to the person before some witnesses. A clear admonition of God to his children to live together in peace and to love each other in spite of our shortcomings can be seen in Paul's letter to the Ephesians in chapter five, from verse twenty-one to verse thirty-three.

Submitting yourselves one to another in the fear of God. Wives, submit yourselves unto your own husbands, as unto the Lord. For the husband is the head of the wife, even as Christ is the head of the church: and he is the saviour of the body. Therefore as the church is subject unto Christ, so let the wives be to their own husbands in everything. Husbands, love your wives, even as Christ also loved the church, and gave himself for it; That he might sanctify and cleanse it with the washing of water by the word, That he might present it to himself a glorious church, not having spot, or wrinkle, or any such thing; but that it should be holy and without blemish. So ought men to love their wives as their own bodies. He that loveth his wife loveth himself. For no man ever yet hated his own flesh; but nourisheth and cherisheth it, even as the Lord the church: For we are members of his body, of his flesh, and of his bones. For this cause shall a man leave his father and mother, and shall be joined unto his wife, and they two shall be one flesh. This is a great mystery: but I speak concerning Christ and the church. Nevertheless let every one of you in particular so love his wife even as himself; and the wife see that she reverence her husband.

When we begin to focus on God's purpose and not on our selfish desires and ambitions it helps us to overlook certain things and we will be able to single out the real issues that are bringing stress on our marriages. We run into problems when we focus on our own will and not on the will of the Father. At a point during his earthly journey Jesus has this recorded about him;

He went a little farther and fell on His face, and prayed, saying, "O My Father, if it is possible, let this cup pass from me; nevertheless, not as I will, but as You will" (Matthew 26:39 NKJV).

Jesus could have said no to the redemption process. In fact he asked the father if he could fashion out a different way, but he added, "Not as I will but as you will".

One of the qualities that endeared David to God's heart was his "heartitude", -my own word for our heart response toward God. To some people their "heartitude" is stubbornness, to some it is arrogance and pride, yet to some it is out right rebellion. But for some, it is reverential fear of God. This was the case with David. He had such a tender heart towards God and was quick to admit his wrong before God and willingly repenting of them. To repent means to turn away from ones sinful ways. Unlike most people today, whenever they are confronted with their sins, they become defensive and give lame excuses to defend themselves instead of repenting of those sins. This was the problem Adam had in the Garden of Eden, when God confronted him with his sin.

And the Lord God called unto Adam, and said unto him, Where art thou? And he said, I heard thy voice in the garden, and I was afraid, because I was naked; and I hid myself. And he said, Who told thee that thou wast naked? Hast thou eaten of the tree, whereof I commanded thee that thou shouldest not eat? (Genesis 3:9-11)

He was quick to respond in verse twelve.

And the man said, The woman whom thou gavest to be with me, she gave me of the tree, and I did eat. The blame game did not start today. The bible says that God desires truth from the heart (Psalm 51:6)

31

CHAPTER THREE

THE CAUSES OF
DIVORCE

The Pharisees also came unto him, tempting him, and saying unto him, Is it lawful for a man to put away his wife for every cause? And he answered and said unto them, Have ye not read, that he which made them at the beginning made them male and female, And said, For this cause shall a man leave father and mother, and shall cleave to his wife: and they twain shall be one flesh? Wherefore they are no more twain, but one flesh. What therefore God hath joined together let not man put asunder (Matthew 19:3-6).

And I say to you, whoever divorces his wife, except for sexual immorality, and marries another, commits adultery; and whoever marries her who is divorced commits adultery" (Matthew 19:9 NKJV).

From the above scriptures it is evidently clear that God intends marriage to be for a life time. Divorce is not an option in God's concept of marriage, it is an exception. However, there are several things that cause people to opt for divorce contrary to God's provision for marriage. For the purpose of this writing I will classify them under the following five groups:

1. ATTACK AND DECEPTION OF THE ENEMY:

We hardly consider the activities of the unseen wicked spiritual realm when it comes to the issue of divorce. This contributes to a large extent to the crisis we see in marriages. This attack comes from the domain of the devil in the unseen supernatural realm. Many people are unaware of the existence of this realm. This makes such people to focus solely on their spouses as the sole source of their problem. They don't do anything to address this realm of operation. Anything that is of God and from God attracts the devil's wrath.

Marriage is one of those things that have the signature of God's approval. As a matter of fact it came from him; it is not man's idea.God brought the woman to the man and joined them together in marriage. Marriage is not a culture or tradition of any nation. It does not belong to any particular race or religion. The devil knows that a God centered home will produce Godly children who will continue the legacy of godliness. More so, the devil has vehemently attacked marriage because it is a picture of the relationship between Christ and the church. Crisis in marriage is not from God. The bible says:

For God is not the author of confusion, but of peace, as in all churches of the saint (1 Corinthians 14:33).

That is, he is not the source of problems in marriage. Marital problem is a form of confusion, created by the devil. Otherwise, how can you explain the situation where a husband and wife that said I love you to each other today becomes avowed enemy a few months down the line. The devil makes you look at your spouse as the source of the problem. Do not believe the lie of the devil.

Your spouse is not the source of the problem, your spouse is not your enemy; your wife is your helper, your enemy is the devil and he is the source of the problem.

The Lord God said, "It is not good for the man to be alone. I will make a helper suitable for him" (Genesis 2:18 NKJV).

The devil will not change nor stop his evil works. He is determined to wreak every marriage. It is his sworn mission to *steal, to kill and to destroy* (John 10:10a). He is the chief architect behind all problems in marriage. The Bible describes him as your adversary.

Be sober, be vigilant; because your adversary the devil, as a roaring lion, walketh about, seeking whom he may devour: Whom resist stedfast in the faith, knowing that the same afflictions are accomplished in your brethren that are in the world (1 Peter 5:8-9).

An adversary is an antagonist. He is the one contending against us in our marriages. As an adversary the devil has determined to fight against us continuously, and relentlessly with this one purpose: to destroy our marriages. The adversary we are dealing with is a formidable adversary. He is hostile and he fights against anything and anyone that represents God. I have good news for you.

But the God of all grace, who hath called us unto his eternal glory by Christ Jesus, after that ye have suffered a while, make you perfect, stablish, strengthen, settle you. (1 Peter 5:10)

And the God of peace shall bruise Satan under your feet shortly. The grace of our Lord Jesus Christ be with you. Amen. (Romans 16:20)

The devil is diabolic, systematic and diplomatic. He will look for the best and most potent weapon to use in his attack. Based on one's disposition and natural tendencies, the enemy knows the right tool he will employ. He will not waste his time using a thing that will not produce any result in his mission: to steal, kill and destroy. He will stop at nothing until he sees husband and wife going against each other. Your wife is not your problem; your husband is not your problem. The devil is the cause of it all. However, many marriages make the devil's job easy by opening the door to him and inviting him in. There are certain things that husbands and wives say and do to each other which give the devil the opportunity to foment problems in homes. The Bible says:

Neither give place to the devil (Ephesians 4:27).

Someone once said, "If you give the devil a foothold he will turn it to a stronghold". The key to keeping him away is not to give him a place in the first place. Quickly come together to resolve any issue you might have. That's why the bible says;

Be ye angry, and sin not: let not the sun go down upon your wrath: (Ephesians 4:26)

Also, the devil deceives people not to believe the word of God. This is one of his greatest assaults on mankind. God's provision for a peaceful marriage is the good news, the gospel of Jesus Christ. Many today have bought into the lie that man wrote the bible, or that the bible has been changed in the course of the translation. Do not believe it. God's word is still the only answer to the crisis of this life, marital or otherwise. I have come across a lot of people (people of color) that believe that Christianity is synonymous with the white. You can hear them say that Christianity is the white man's religion. The fact that the Whiteman discovered the gospel earlier than most of us is a privilege; it does not make it theirs. Salvation does not belong to America; the Bible says that salvation is of the Jews (John 4:22). I really thank God for the sacrifices the Whiteman made and are still making, and the prices they paid in spreading the gospel of Jesus Christ. No one's salvation is superior or inferior to another. We are born again by the same Holy Spirit and have all been accepted in the beloved. My favorite program on Trinity Broadcasting Networks (TBN) is the Billy Graham classics. I always pray with the program that God should not let his sacrifice for this nation be in vain.

2. IGNORANCE AND LACK OF
   PREPARATION:

My people are destroyed for lack of knowledge: because thou hast rejected knowledge, I will also reject thee, that thou shalt be no priest to me:

seeing thou hast forgotten the law of thy God, I will also forget thy children   (Hosea 4:6)

A lot of people are ignorant of the marriage covenant. All they know is that marriage is a contract. No one has explained to them the implication of being married. They do not understand that entering into the marital relationship comes with its attendant responsibilities. Think about this, all the years you spent in pursuit of academic career, from pre-K to post graduate, not a fraction of a second was spent to teach you or train you on how to live with a man or a woman as a husband or as a wife as the case may be. Yet, you are expected to spend your entire life in that marriage relationship. We do a lot of things based on assumptions and what we see on the big screen and what we see people do around us. Stop and think! The models you see on the big screen are playing make belief, acting as it were. Ask yourself, are they married? Are they living with their spouses? Living together with a man or a woman and sleeping together is not equal to marriage. There is a supernatural dimension that is factored in, the moment a man and a woman are pronounced husband and wife.

This is what makes for the emotional trauma and pain that people go through when they divorce, because divorce is a spiritual amputation without anesthetics. Wisdom demands that you seek for knowledge on the subject of marriage. You need godly counsel. Do not jump into marriage without adequate preparation. If you jump into it you will be quick to jump out. I was listening to a preacher on the radio, speaking about marriage. He said that marriage is like the insects on the window screen in a room with light bulb on. Those that are inside want to get out and those that are outside want to get in. The fact that you are of age to marry is not the same as preparation to marry. You can be of age and yet have not done one bit of preparation. Preparation begins with you as a person and it is your responsibility. Hear this; marriage is a responsibility not a child's play. I read from the Dallas Morning News not too long ago the story of a young man that beat his infant baby to death. According to the story, it was simply because he came back from his job and needed to sleep and the baby was crying and would not let him sleep. What a tragedy! Obviously he was not prepared for the responsibility of fatherhood. Marriage requires your taking up your responsibilities and being committed to it for it to succeed. It can be likened to a garden; you weed it and add manure so that you can eat the fruit of it.

The preparations of the heart in man, and the answer of the tongue, is from the Lord (Proverbs 16:1).

So Jotham became mighty, because he prepared his ways before the Lord his God (2 Chronicles 27:6).

A man that hath friends must shew himself friendly: and there is a friend that sticketh closer than a brother (Proverbs 18:24).

It is unfortunate that we prepare virtually for every venture in life; this we call due diligence, but not much is done when it comes to marriage, which happens to be one of the most critical aspects of one's life. We even prepare for wedding but not the marriage. A successful wedding does not connote a successful marriage. Neither does the cost of a wedding guarantee the success of the marriage. Hear what Jesus said:

For which of you, intending to build a tower, does not sit down first and count the cost, whether he has enough to finish it (Luke 14:28).

The tower speaks of an enduring and lasting structure. It is not something you build today and the next day you want to rebuild it. Marriage can be considered as that tower in this respect because it is meant to last till death.

So much of divorce we have today largely depends on lack of adequate preparation. Preparing for wedding is not the same with preparing for marriage. Wedding is a one-time event whereas marriage is a lifetime adventure. Marriage begins where wedding ends. Marriage is not for boys and girls.

Therefore shall a man leave his father and his mother, and shall cleave unto his wife: and they shall be one flesh (Genesis 2:24).

This is not just talking about physical maturity alone but most importantly, spiritual and emotional maturity. I remember a story that one of my teachers told us in our singles' fellowship during one of our singles' convention. He was talking on preparing for marriage. According to his story, there was this man that came home under the rain only to discover that his house was flooded. He met the wife crying because of the damage the flood has caused in their home and he joined the wife and started crying as well. Then he, our teacher, added, their teardrops were increasing the volume of water in the house. Maturity and wisdom will make one to take the right steps in any given situation. Preparation is personal responsibility. Success in marriage does not begin with finding the right person; it begins with you becoming the right person.

A man that hath friends must shew himself friendly: and there is a friend that sticketh closer than a brother (Proverbs 18:24).

Equip and prepare yourself. Read books that deal with emotions and learn how to control them. One of the things preparation does for a person is that it makes one to know the right steps to take at the appropriate time. There is nothing that comes up that takes you unaware. The fact that you are reading this book is an indication of your commitment to your marital success. Cultivate the fruit of the Spirit as revealed in the scriptures in the book of Galatians chapter five in verse twenty-two and practice them.

But the fruit of the Spirit is love, joy, peace, longsuffering, gentleness, goodness, faith Meekness, temperance: against such there is no law.

Also, you need a good and reliable source of income. But, let your trust be in God as your ultimate source and your provider. When you enter into marriage unprepared, it becomes easy for you to check out when problems come. Don't make any provision for a second marriage; believe it that this is your first and last marriage till death does you part. Part of the preparation for marriage should include learning to forgive. Whatever may be the cause of the problem anyone will encounter in marriage, the ultimate desire of the devil is to get you offended and make you not to forgive. Not forgiving your spouse will produce bitterness and bitterness will trouble your marriage. Trouble in marriage can lead to divorce if not handled carefully.

Looking diligently lest any man fail of the grace of God; lest any root of bitterness springing up trouble you, and thereby many be defiled (Hebrews 12:15).

A lot of people come into their marriage with a preconceived idea of how their spouses should behave. They have the notion that they can make their spouse behave in a certain way they want, as if their spouses are robots or as if they have the power to change any human being. They talk; they nag, all in the bid to control their spouse. When they don't succeed at their manipulations, they become enraged and will do anything to frustrate their spouse. Unknown to them, they are attacking their marriage.

Making up one's mind is part of the preparation. From the onset, before you step into marriage you must make up your mind that this is your only and last marriage till death. Don't enter into a marriage relationship with the mindset of trying it out if it will work. In today's culture people enter into marriage with a prenuptial agreement written out. It is easy for people to swing if their mind is not made up in the beginning. The book of Psalms declares;

My heart is fixed, O God, my heart is fixed: I will sing and give praise (Psalms 57:7).

If your heart is made up you can live with your spouse as long as you live. You will not be swayed by any problem that comes the way of your marriage.

Pray and ask God to guide you as you embark on this journey of preparation. The time of courtship is the time to validate one another not the time to sleep with each other. This is a time of getting to know your "would be" spouse better. It is the time to study him or her, his or her emotions, temperament, perspective to life, position with God, reaction to issues, and many more.

3. MISPLACED GRACE

I want to take a little time here to talk about grace. The way some believers talk about the word grace it appears as if grace is an idle word. It gives the impression that grace absolves one of any responsibility towards God. Grace is a living word; it is the power of God at work in the life of a mortal man. It is an active force from God to enable one do things that are humanly difficult. The message of eternal salvation has not been properly communicated; so people assume that grace will make up for their lack of commitment to the demands of the scriptures. They do not show any sense of obligation towards God. Grace is not a license to live a wayward life, nor is it a permission to live a life of sin. In his counsel to Moses in the book of Exodus chapter eighteen in verse twenty, Jethro made this profound statement to him:

And thou shalt teach them ordinances and laws, and shalt shew them the way wherein they must walk, and the work that they must do.

In other words, teach them the word of God to communicate to them how they ought to live and their obligations as children of God.

What shall we say then? Shall we continue in sin, that grace may abound? God forbid. How shall we, that are dead to sin, live any longer therein? (Romans 6:1-2)

One of the major works of grace after one is born again is to make one say no to ungodly living. Divorce and remarry contrary to God's word is ungodly living, adultery and fornication is ungodly living, bitterness and anger is ungodly living, and so on. Grace is an enablement to live a life of obedience to God.

For by grace are ye saved through faith; and that not of yourselves: it is the gift of God (Ephesians 2:8).

For the grace of God that bringeth salvation hath appeared to all men, teaching us that, denying ungodliness and worldly lusts, we should live soberly, righteously, and godly, in this present world (Titus 2:11-12).

Grace places a responsibility on you as a child of God. Just the same way faith is authenticated by your works, that is, your corresponding action towards the word of God, there should be evidence that you have received the grace of God. Otherwise the grace you received is in vain. Hear what the apostle James said:

Even so faith, if it hath not works, is dead, being alone. Yea, a man may say, Thou hast faith, and I have works: shew me thy faith without thy works, and I will shew thee my faith by my works. Thou believest that there is one God; thou doest well: the devils also believe, and tremble. But wilt thou know, O vain man, that faith without works is dead? (James 2:17-20)

The apostle Paul corroborated this fact in the following scripture:

But by the grace of God I am what I am: and his grace which was bestowed upon me was not in vain; but I laboured more abundantly than they all: yet not I, but the grace of God which was with me (1 Corinthians 15:10).

We are not saved by works but our works show that we have obtained grace. John the Baptist said to the Pharisees and Sadducees to *"bear fruits worthy of repentance"* (Matthew 3:8). Grace is not a license for laziness. In the above scripture Paul said "I laboured". The word laboured connotes exertion of energy, paying the required price for grace to have its way. We go to the gym to workout in order to maintain our physical bodies, for our bodies to be in shape. So also, we ought to workout in our marriages. There are things we ought to be doing and there are things we ought not to be doing in order to maintain our marriages. Note the things that upset your spouse and try not to do them, and the things that make him or her happy, go out of your way to do them. Every building enterprise requires an effort. Buildings don't drop from heaven. In case you see one please let me know.

For every house is built by someone, but He who built all things is God (Hebrews 3:4 NKJV).

Many people today claim to be followers of Jesus Christ but they are not willing to abide by his word. If you are truly a child of God you don't make your own rules, you don't pick and choose the word of God you will obey and the ones you will not obey. Through the grace of God we have become bond servants of Christ, no longer to do things our own way, that in all things he might take preeminence. Following Christ is a life-long commitment. You follow him in season and out of season, not when it is convenient for you. Jesus said,

"Take my yoke upon you, and learn of me; for I am meek and lowly in heart: and ye shall find rest unto your souls. For my yoke is easy, and my burden is light (Matthew 11:29-30).

Many do not want to take the yoke of Christ because they think it will put a restriction on them and become an impediment to their way of living. What is the yoke of Christ? It is complete obedience to the commands of the scriptures. The truth is that the yoke of Christ most often than not is contrary to our natural way of responding to issues. However, it will keep you from doing things that will hurt your life both now and hereafter. His yoke is an expression of pure love and true liberty. Why do people think it incredible in this time and age that one can live with his or her spouse throughout their life time? I cannot divorce my wife even if I want to. Under no circumstance will I do that, because the yoke of Christ constrains me. I made this commitment to the Lord, that I will not play any role in anyone's divorce. I will not be a part of it and my name will not be mentioned in such cases.

4.   GREED AND WRONG MOTIVES:

You must ask yourself the soul searching question, why do I want to get married to this person. If you can't find your "why", or your "why" is only based on material gains or on sex, then you are marrying for the wrong reason. There are people that entered into the marital relationship with the wrong motives, their sole reason being material gains. They have selfish ambitions which they intend to pursue through that marriage. These are gold diggers. They marry their spouse because of what they want to get. They place their ambition above their marriage and careless about the welfare of their marriage. Some are driven by greed; they want material gains in terms of alimony, child support and their share of the common property. As a child of God you must view things from the lens of the scriptures. God thinks in terms of posterity, that is the future generations that will come from that marriage, not just the two of you involved. That should be our baseline when deciding on the choice of spouse. What kind of generation do you want to come from you? If you desire a godly generation then godliness should be your guide in your decision making. If you get married to a person that has no fear of God do not expect to raise a godly generation.

And did not he make one? Yet had he the residue of the spirit. And wherefore one? That he might seek a godly seed. Therefore take heed to your spirit, and let none deal treacherously against the wife of his youth. (Malachi 2:15)

5. LACK OF AGREEMENT

Can two walk together, except they be agreed? (Amos 3:3)

The main reason why God forbids inter-faith marriage is because it works against the first level, and the most important form of agreement, which is spiritual agreement. If there is no spiritual agreement between both spouses, the tendency for conflict and crisis is at the highest level. It doesn't matter how much you claim to love each other, there is problem already waiting to manifest because you are building on a faulty foundation. With a faulty foundation, you are helpless.

If the foundations be destroyed, what can the righteous do? (Psalm 11:3).

Concerning the daughters of Zelophehad Moses the servant of the Lord made the following statement,

And Moses commanded the children of Israel according to the word of the LORD, saying, The tribe of the sons of Joseph hath said well. This is the thing which the LORD doth command concerning the daughters of Zelophehad, saying, Let them marry to whom they think best; only to the family of the tribe of their father shall they marry (Numbers 36:5-6).

The family here, in our time, speaks of our faith family. Inter-faith marriage is like putting "a square peg in a round hole". It does not work period.

We live in a world where humans think that they are wiser than God their maker. In today's culture, God will be labeled a bigot. As a matter of fact any one that takes a stand based on God's word is called such name. Lack of spiritual agreement is by far the greatest factor that contributes to problems in the marital relationship. The other aspect of agreement is the physical agreement. When both spouses are not in agreement it creates problems that negatively impact almost everything they do in that marriage. The physical agreement speaks of compromise. The two spouses must agree on how they intend to run the family. By virtue of the marriage covenant everything owned by each of the spouse prior to their marriage belongs to both of them now that they are married. No one should say that any of the things he or she owned before getting married is his or hers. They should have all things in common. That is the way it ought to be according to the word of God; *"and they shall be one flesh"* (Genesis 2:24). However, not everyone has come to the level of this understanding. So you need to sit down and plan together how you want things to be done in your family. There should not be any unilateral decision without proper explanation. There are identical twins but there is no identical marriage. Every marriage is unique. That is why it does not make any sense to insist on a particular way of doing things in your marriage just because that is what you saw in a particular marriage, maybe your parents'. You have to agree on what will work best for your marriage and you both agree on that. Don't run your marriage based on assumption that he or she will understand why you did some things in a certain way. You have to communicate with each other. There is a difference between communication and instruction.

Communication is two-way traffic while instruction is one-way traffic. It is of utmost importance that you take time to discuss critical issues that constitute potential trigger of disagreement. Taking care of such issues will minimize conflict in those directions. When nothing is done to take care of such issues it will lead to finger pointing, then it escalates to major problems. Money is becoming a major player in the issue of disagreement in marriage and as such should be duly discussed. There must be agreement on how you spend your money. You must agree on whether to keep joint account or separate accounts. You can keep a personal account but don't keep a secret account. Don't engage in any transaction, financial or otherwise without discussing it with your spouse. God is watching you. Do not deal deceitfully with your spouse.

The eyes of the Lord are in every place, beholding the evil and the good (Proverbs 15:3).

CHAPTER FOUR

CONDITIONS FOR
REMARRYING

The scriptures made it clear that God hates divorce.

For the Lord, the God of Israel, saith that he hateth putting away: for one covereth violence with his garment, saith the Lord of hosts: therefore take heed to your spirit, that ye deal not treacherously (Malachi 2:16).

Paul was emphatic corroborating with prophet Malachi when he said,

"And unto the married I command, yet not I, but the Lord, Let not the wife depart from her husband" (1 Corinthians 7:10).

This is because divorce is contrary to God's plan. God's plan for marriage is one man and one woman for life, nothing should separate them.

Wherefore they are no more twain, but one flesh. What therefore God hath joined together, let not man put asunder (Matthew 19:6).

Divorce is what the devil wants for us. He wants every marriage to end in divorce and be entered into the divorce record database. Your marriage will not end up there in Jesus name. From God's concept of marriage, divorce does not end a marriage. In the eyes of the Lord you are still married to that man or woman. No power on this earth can annul the verdict of God. Jesus said that anyone that divorces and remarries, except for some well spelt out reasons in the word of God is committing adultery.

And I say unto you, Whosoever shall put away his wife, except it be for fornication, and shall marry another, committeth adultery: and whoso marrieth her which is put away doth commit adultery (Matthew 19:9).

The world is making light the issue of divorce and remarry, and has made it part of the culture. The church is now infested with the virus of divorces and remarries. Many preachers are culprits of this scriptural violation and as such cannot condemn such ungodly practices in the church. Instead, they are the ones that encourage people to get divorced. From Jesus' words in the gospel of Mark chapter ten in verse twenty-eight through to verse thirty, it implies that even if you love him (Jesus) so much and you are so much committed to do his works that it cost you your marriage in divorce, you are not permitted to remarry. Take a close look at that passage of the scripture below you will notice that he omitted two things when he was mentioning the thing you will receive back for what you gave up for his sake and the gospel's. He did not include father and wife as part of what you will receive for what you gave up. He left out father because he takes up that role in your life (Psalm 27:10), and he left out wife because that was not part of the conditions to remarry.

Then Peter began to say unto him, Lo, we have left all, and have followed thee. And Jesus answered and said, Verily I say unto you, There is no man that hath left house, or brethren, or sisters, or father, or mother, or wife, or children, or lands, for my sake, and the gospel's, But he shall receive an hundredfold now in this time, houses, and brethren, and sisters, and mothers, and children, and lands, with persecutions; and in the world to come eternal life (Mark 10:28-30).

If losing one's marriage in the course of doing God's work does not give one the right to remarry, read on to find out the conditions under which remarrying is allowed in the word of God.

DEATH OF A SPOUSE

Life is an irreplaceable gift from God. There is no spare life, neither is there any artificial life. You cannot buy life; it is a free gift from God. That's why we should be grateful to God for the gift of life and we should cherish it and not destroy it, like we see all over the world today. A lot of people are blind to the goodness of God in their lives, that's why they complain instead of giving God thanks. They don't know that outside of salvation, the greatest gift in life is the gift of life. A dead person can do absolutely nothing. Of what good is it to anyone that he or she owns hundreds of billions of dollars and he or she is dead? The irony of it all is that he or she is not going with a dime to where he or she is going. It is a painful thing to lose a loved one to death. In fact God calls death, an enemy (1 Corinthians 15:26). Death creates a vacuum in a home; it brings separation, sorrow and pain. The truth is that, it is absolutely difficult if not impossible to estimate the impact of the death of a loved one. As painful as it may be, it is expected that one should move on with life after the death of a loved one. It is okay to mourn the loss of a loved one, but one should not allow the grief to overwhelm him or her, especially if you are a child of God because you will re-unite with your loved one at the end. There are people that carry the pain and grief of the death of a loved one longer than necessary. Such sorrow of heart can affect ones health. I pray that God will give us long life in Jesus name.

When ones spouse dies, he or she becomes eligible to remarry. He or she can remarry if he or she chooses to, without violating God's law. Let's go to the bible, the manual of life and hear from the author of marriage:

For the woman who has a husband is bound by the law to her husband as long as he lives. But if the husband dies, she is released from the law of her husband. So then if, while her husband lives, she marries another man, she will be called an adulteress; but if her husband dies, she is free from that law, so that she is no adulteress, though she has married another man (Romans 7:2-3 NKJV).

I say therefore to the unmarried and widows, it is good for them if they abide even as I. But if they cannot contain, let them marry: for it is better to marry than to burn (1 Corinthians 7:8-9).

SEXUAL PROMISCUITY

When one of the two spouses is given to sexual promiscuity, it is a legal ground to divorce and remarry without violating God's law. Even a harlot when he or she is married it is expected that he or she should curb the excesses of extramarital affairs. The worst sin you can commit against your wife or husband is marital infidelity. When sexual promiscuity becomes a habit that is obvious, you can't hide it anymore, not even from your spouse, he or she has a legal ground before God to get a divorce. That is, to say, when you fragrantly violate God's law and defile your marriage bed, you are asking for a divorce. One of the reasons for marriage is to avoid illegitimate sex.

And I say to you, whoever divorces his wife, except for sexual immorality, and marries another, commits adultery; and whoever marries her who is divorced commits adultery." (Matthew 19:9 NKJV).

Although sexual immoralities is a legal ground for divorce and remarry from God's perspective, one does better when he or she forgives his or her spouse from the heart and continues in the marriage. It is a sign of love and maturity and it is an honor to God. God will surely reward you.

WHEN UNBELIEVING SPOUSE DEPARTS

Yet another condition for remarriage according to God's word is when an unbelieving spouse departs. This happens when people marry as unbelievers. In other words, the man and the woman got married when neither of them knew the Lord. If, in the course of their marriage, in the process of time, one of them receives the Lord Jesus as his or her personal Lord and savior and the other decides to leave as a result of that, the other spouse can remarry if he or she chooses to and yet does not violate the law of God.

Now to the married I command, yet not I but the Lord: A wife is not to depart from her husband. But even if she does depart, let her remain unmarried or be reconciled to her husband. And a husband is not to divorce his wife. But to the rest I, not the Lord, say: If any brother has a wife who does not believe, and she is willing to live with him, let him not divorce her. And a woman who has a husband, who does not believe, if he is willing to live with her, let her not divorce him. For the unbelieving husband is sanctified by the wife, and the unbelieving wife is sanctified by the husband; otherwise your children would be unclean, but now they are holy. But if the unbeliever departs, let him depart; a brother or a sister is not under bondage in such cases. But God has called us to peace. (1 Corinthians 7:10-15 NKJV).

There are instances where people have deceived the unsuspecting spouse by pretending to be born again. If any of the two withholds some vital information which will make for impediment to their being joined together in marriage, that marriage is illegal. Take for example, someone that has had a previous marriage and does not disclose that to a "would be" spouse prior to their marriage, that marriage is illegal. The person that joined you in marriage is not a factor when it comes to the legitimacy of any marriage. The only factor to be considered is what God said.

When a person remarries outside of these conditions it is stealing a woman or a man as the case may be. When a person steals something, no matter how long he or she keeps the item with him or her, it does not make it his or hers. The person is simply a thief. That being said, you can imagine how many thieves we have around. The law of God says

"Thou shall not steal" (Exodus 20:15).

The book of Exodus chapter twenty is where you find the Ten Commandments. Now let's take a look at verse seventeen.

"You shall not covet your neighbor's house; you shall not covet your neighbor's wife, nor his male servant, nor his female servant, nor his ox, nor his donkey, nor anything that is your neighbor's.

Don't desire to have another man's wife or another woman's husband. Don't do it. Jesus was discussing with the woman at the well and they got to this point,

"Jesus said to her, "Go, call your husband, and come here." The woman answered and said, "I have no husband." Jesus said to her, "You have well said, 'I have no husband,' for you have had five husbands, and the one whom you now have is not your husband; in that you spoke truly." (John 4:16-18 NKJV).

Could it be that you are living with a man that is not your husband or a woman that is not your wife? You need to find out. What I am saying might be going against the grain of your belief but receive it with meekness because it is the truth of God's word. Ask God for grace to take the necessary steps to make amend where necessary. The only genuine and irrefutable factor that authenticates ones love for Christ is obedience to his word.

If ye love me, keep my commandments (John 14:15).

Then said Jesus to those Jews which believed on him, If ye continue in my word, then are ye my disciples indeed (John 8:31).

There is no substitute to obedience in the kingdom of God. Saul the king of Israel wanted to substitute obedience with sacrifice and ended up losing his throne as the king.

And Samuel said, Hath the Lord as great delight in burnt offerings and sacrifices, as in obeying the voice of the Lord? Behold, to obey is better than sacrifice, and to hearken than the fat of rams (1 Samuel 15:22).

If you need to take any action do so now. Actions are the proof of change.

While it is said, Today if ye will hear his voice, harden not your hearts, as in the provocation (Hebrews 3:15).

CHAPTER FIVE

SETTLING DISPUTES

Problem in marriage can be likened to problem in a passenger plane. It doesn't matter who is the cause of the problem, everyone onboard is impacted.

Dispute or disagreement creates a division and a separation between husband and wife. It makes them to turn their back to each other. It brings hindrance to the progress of the family and it negative impacts everything they do.

Now I beseech you, brethren, by the name of our Lord Jesus Christ, that ye all speak the same thing, and that there be no divisions among you; but that ye be perfectly joined together in the same mind and in the same judgment (1 Corinthians 1:10).

Jesus said that offenses are unavoidable. The only option that is left to us is to learn how to deal with it. So, we "disagree to agree", says a popular saying. It is my desire Spirit of God will use this chapter to put a handle on the subject of offense so that you will be able to handle it whenever you encounter one.

[Jesus Warns of Offenses] Then He said to the disciples, "It is impossible that no offenses should come, but woe to him through whom they do come! (Luke 17:1 NKJV)

We don't abandon our cars because it has problem. We go to see a doctor or a specialist when we are sick. We look for a fix for virtually everything in life. But when we have issues with our marriages so many people abandon their marriages. The same way we take our cars to the dealership or go see a specialist for health issues, we ought to take our marital issues to God. He is the one that made marriage and he can fix it if there is any problem. Simply ask him in prayer to help you and he will help you. There is hope for your marriage no matter how bad you think things are right now, God can and will turn it around for good.

For there is hope of a tree, if it be cut down, that it will sprout again, and that the tender branch thereof will not cease. Though the root thereof wax old in the earth, and the stock thereof die in the ground; Yet through the scent of water it will bud, and bring forth boughs like a plant (Job 14:7-9).

Problem in marriage is not a strange phenomenon. I don't know of any marriage that has not encountered one form of problem or the other. Any married couple that will be honest will attest to this fact. Do not think that what you are going through in your marriage is unbearable. If everyone should walk away from their marriages because of the difficulties they are having in the marriage, I can guarantee this; we will not have a single marriage standing today. Hear what the apostle Peter had to say:

"Beloved, think it not strange concerning the fiery trial which is to try you, as though some

strange thing happened unto you" (1Peter 4:12).... *"knowing that the same afflictions are accomplished in your brethren that are in the world* (1Peter 5:9b).

Husband and wife stay together in marriage not because they are compatible, like jigsaw puzzle pieces that perfectly fit into each other. They stayed in their marriage because of their commitment to God and to their marriage. As humans offenses are inevitable. Whether you like it or not you are going to have them, either you offend someone or you are offended. When one is offended he or she cannot hide it. You will see it on the face, or hear it from the voice or see it through the person's actions. Anyone carrying offenses cannot smile or be joyful in a relationship. Don't ignore offenses; deal with them as quickly as possible.

Moreover if thy brother shall trespass against thee, go and tell him his fault between thee and him alone: if he shall hear thee, thou hast gained thy brother (Matthew 18:15).

Applying this same principle to our marriage, if your husband or you wife, whichever is the case, offends you, go to him or her and talk it over with him or her. There are many potential triggers of problems in marriage. These include but not limited to gender differences, differences in perception, differences in background, differences in opinion, life experiences, infidelity, and many more. These are obvious sources of conflicts in marriage. Also, money is becoming one of the biggest threats to peace in homes today. As a result of this there should be proper discussion and agreement on the issue of money.

A long time ago God had a dispute with man because man disregarded and disobeyed his command. God turned away from man and man could not reach God. During this period there was a long silence between God and man. After some time God decided to reach out to man and to reconcile with him. He sent his servants the apostles and the prophets to mediate between him and man. The apostles and the prophets could not resolve the issue. They could not forgive the sin of man. Finally, God came by himself to man in the person of Jesus Christ to reconcile man unto himself.

To wit, that God was in Christ, reconciling the world unto himself, not imputing their trespasses unto them; and hath committed unto us the word of reconciliation (2 Corinthians 5:19).

The only way God could reconcile with man was through forgiveness of sin through the shedding of the blood of his dear son, Jesus Christ. The bedrock of the work of redemption is forgiveness. Drawing a parallel from this, one can confidently say that the key to settling disputes is not identifying who is wrong or who is right, but being able to forgive your spouse from your heart not from your lips. Just as Christ sacrificed his life to reconcile us to God, at least one of the spouses must play the sacrificial role in the marriage. He or she must willingly sacrifice his or her rights for the sake of peace and unity. The key of forgiveness is the greatest asset in resolving disputes. Keep this key with you so as not to be locked out of your marriage. Many couples are spiritually locked out of their marriages simply because they are not willing to forgive. One of the signs that one is locked out of his or her marriage is inability to fellowship and relate together as husband and wife. In the book of Matthew chapter eighteen, beginning from verse twenty-three to verse thirty-five, Jesus taught a lesson on forgiveness by telling a story.

Therefore is the kingdom of heaven likened unto a certain king, which would take account of his servants. And when he had begun to reckon, one was brought unto him, which owed him ten thousand talents. But forasmuch as he had not to pay, his lord commanded him to be sold, and his wife, and children, and all that he had, and payment to be made. The servant therefore fell down, and worshipped him, saying, Lord, have patience with me, and I will pay thee all. Then the lord of that servant was moved with compassion, and loosed him, and forgave him the debt. But the same servant went out, and found one of his fellowservants, which owed him an hundred pence: and he laid hands on him, and took him by the throat, saying, Pay me that thou owest. And his fellowservant fell down at his feet, and besought him, saying, Have patience with me, and I will pay thee all. And he would not: but went and cast him into prison, till he should pay the debt. So when his fellowservants saw what was done, they were very sorry, and came and told unto their lord all that was done. Then his lord, after that he had called him, said unto him, O thou wicked servant, I forgave thee all that debt, because thou desiredst me: Shouldest not thou also have had compassion on thy fellowservant, even as I had pity on thee? And his lord was wroth, and delivered him to the tormentors, till he should pay all that was due unto him. So likewise shall my heavenly Father do also unto you, if ye from your hearts forgive not every one his brother their trespasses.

He ended that story by saying that if you don't forgive people from your heart, that God will not forgive you. Learn to forgive. Some offenses can be painful but God says forgive. Do not bottle up offense. That can be dangerous. Not only does offense cause problem in the marriage, many sicknesses and many undiagnosed sicknesses can be traceable to offense. Offense is a direct attack on the heart, and the heart is a very strategic organ in the human anatomy. Unknown to many, they are hemorrhaging inside their heart because of the pain caused them by their spouse or by someone else. If only you can understand and receive the message of forgiveness, I can guarantee this; over ninety percent of the problem is solved. Forgiveness is the crux of the whole matter when it comes to the issue of settling disputes in any relationship.

Forbearing one another, and forgiving one another, if any man have a quarrel against any: even as Christ forgave you, so also do ye (Colossians 3:13).

God made provision for involving other people in conflict resolution if both spouses could not resolve the issue themselves. This is the principle of escalation in conflict resolution. Do not hesitate to employ it if you have to. I have used it when there was need for me to do so. Get help when you need it, do not wait until things get out of hands. Dealing with conflict is not easy, especially in marriage. Confide with your pastor or a mature child of God with proven integrity who will prayerfully counsel you thereby brokering peace.

Moreover if thy brother shall trespass against thee, go and tell him his fault between thee and him alone: if he shall hear thee, thou hast gained thy brother. But if he will not hear thee, then take with thee one or two more, that in the mouth of two or three witnesses every word may be established (Matthew 18:15-16).

As a child of God one ought to study his or her Bible and follow God's instruction. God wants to speak to you concerning any issue that is going on in your life, but how can He speak to you when you don't study your Bible. Hearing from a man of God cannot compare with hearing from God. The bible is self-anointed and is more anointed than any man of God. I am not in any way demeaning the office of the ministers of the gospel; I am also a servant of Christ. I speak the truth in love and the Spirit bears me witness. The woman at the well in the gospel of John chapter four told the people: *Come, see a man, which told me all things that ever I did: is not this the Christ?* – John 4:29 and after the people came and heard from Christ they replied to the woman: *And said unto the woman, Now we believe, not because of thy saying: for we have heard him ourselves, and know that this is indeed the Christ, the Saviour of the world.* – John 4:42. The place of the study of God's word cannot be overemphasized. The answers we are looking for are in the word of God, the way to peace we are looking for is in his word. He is the way, the truth and the life (John 14:6); no one can experience lasting peace without him. He is the prince of peace – Isaiah 9:6

Sometime ago my wife and I had some sharp misunderstanding and we were arguing over certain issues. The verbal confrontation was so much that it appeared as if we were throwing punches at each other. One day I was studying the book of Galatians and I came across this passage in chapter five verses fifteen which reads: *"But if you bite and devour one another, beware lest you be consumed by one another!"* Since that encounter with the word I made the choice to refrain from talking back no matter how provocative her actions or words might be. However, being human, I have fallen short of that on a few occasions. We are not there yet but we are getting better by the day. It is one thing to study the word of God, but a different to apply it. It does not matter how much of the word of God you know, if you don't put them to practice you will not see any change. The profiting of the word of God is in practicing the instructions. Jesus said,

If any man will do his will, he shall know of the doctrine, whether it be of God, or whether I speak of myself (John 7:17).

James said this way:

But be ye doers of the word, and not hearers only, deceiving your own selves (James 1:22).

The devil wants to sustain confusion and argument in homes so that he can continue his evil work. Be wise, and say no to him. Honestly speaking when you engage in biting and devouring one another you are tearing apart the fabrics of your marriage without knowing. You cannot change your spouse by screaming and yelling. Pray, pray, pray.

One more important thing I need to mention in the issue of settling dispute is the role of the mouth. Avoid the wrong use of your mouth.

Whoso keepeth his mouth and his tongue keepeth his soul from troubles (Proverbs 21:23).

When one is offended or provoked, the natural tendency is to respond in the direction of the provocation. The bible calls for restraint when it comes to the use of our tongues. The point of anger is not a good time to respond. The following verses of scripture will help us in understanding how to and how not to use our mouth and our tongue in relating to one another.

Even so the tongue is a little member, and boasteth great things. Behold, how great a matter a little fire kindleth! And the tongue is a fire, a world of iniquity: so is the tongue among our members, that it defileth the whole body, and setteth on fire the course of nature; and it is set on fire of hell (James 3:5-6).

Wherefore, my beloved brethren, let every man be swift to hear, slow to speak, slow to wrath (James 1:19).

A soft answer turneth away wrath: but grievous words stir up anger (Proverbs 15:1).

Let your speech be always with grace, seasoned with salt, that ye may know how ye ought to answer every man (Colossians 4:6).

One of my teachers told us this story about a woman that has serious crisis in her marriage. The woman and the husband fight and curse out themselves. One day she decided to get some help. She went to the church and spoke with the Reverend about the issue. After counseling her, the Reverend gave her a bottle containing a clear liquid and instructed her to take a little of that liquid and hold in her mouth any time the husband starts up an argument. The Reverend told her not to swallow the liquid but to spit it out at the end after the husband has finished all he wants to say trying to provoke an argument. The woman went home and put that to practice and to her amazement, the husband apologized to her after several attempts to provoke her to quarrelling and she did not utter a word. Peace was restored to her home. Praise God! The clear liquid was ordinary water, yes you guessed right. The mouth has been a major cause of the problem. We need to pray like the psalmist;

Set a watch, O Lord, before my mouth; keep the door of my lips (Psalms 141:3).

CHAPTER SIX

THE PLACE OF LOVE

For God so loved the world, that he gave his only begotten Son, that whosoever believeth in him should not perish, but have everlasting life (John 3:16).

But God commendeth his love toward us, in that, while we were yet sinners, Christ died for us (Romans 5:8).

God demonstrated to us what true love is. What we see in the world today is not love at all. What we see in the world today as love can best be described as lust of selfish love, if that is love at all. This is the kind of love that gives in exchange for what it will get. There is a difference between an act of love and a heart of love. What you see most of the time in the world is the act of love. From the above passages of scripture it is evidently clear that God's love is totally different from man's kind of love. God's love does not depend on our performance. It is unconditional love, the agape love. The book of first Corinthians chapter thirteen reveals the characteristics of God's kind of love. I call it the x-ray of love because it reveals the nature of love.

Though I speak with the tongues of men and of angels, but have not love, I have become sounding brass or a clanging cymbal. And though I have the gift of prophecy, and understand all mysteries and all knowledge, and though I have all faith, so that I could remove mountains, but have not love, I am nothing. And though I bestow all my goods to feed the poor, and though I give my body to be burned, but have not love, it profits me nothing. Love suffers long and is kind; love does not envy; love does not parade itself, is not puffed up; does not behave rudely, does not seek its own, is not provoked, thinks no evil; does not rejoice in iniquity, but rejoices in the truth; bears all things, believes all things, hopes all things, endures all things. Love never fails. But whether there are prophecies, they will fail; whether there are tongues, they will cease; whether there is knowledge, it will vanish away.

For we know in part and we prophesy in part. But when that which is perfect has come, then that which is in part will be done away. When I was a child, I spoke as a child, I understood as a child, I thought as a child; but when I became a man, I put away childish things. For now we see in a mirror, dimly, but then face to face. Now I know in part, but then I shall know just as I also am known. And now abide faith, hope, love, these three; but the greatest of these is love

If anyone claims to have love and that love does not line up with the above passage, that kind of love is fake. True love is not what we merely express in our words by saying "I love you". That is just a little part of it. The bulk of what makes up true love is what we do. The language of love, as we say it today, is not English language or Spanish or any other language. You don't need any language to express true love. True love makes a statement without speaking a word. True love is sacrificial; it is giving and not demanding. True love does not look for what it will get in return for what it is giving. One of the major characteristics of a lasting love is endurance. What you are willing to do for your spouse is an indication of your love for him or her. When you truly love your spouse, you look out for his or her interest; you don't do anything that will hurt him or her emotionally or otherwise.

There is a command in scripture for men to love their wives. The word "husband" in that passage is gender specific. This is because men in their normal condition, by nature have strong affinity for women. They have the tendency to give their love to any woman that gets close to them in any relationship. You must have had stories of some men marrying their secretaries or even their nannies. It is not because they want to, the issue I mentioned is their problem. When a man does not have a solid relationship with God he is helpless. God help your men, that we might not fail you. Amen! But, God wants that love to be exclusively reserved for the wife. It does not mean that the man cannot show love to others.

[21] submitting to one another in the fear of God. [22] Wives, submit to your own husbands, as to the Lord. [23] For the husband is head of the wife, as also Christ is head of the church; and He is the Savior of the body. [24] Therefore, just as the church is subject to Christ, so let the wives be to their own husbands in everything. [25] Husbands, love your wives, just as Christ also loved the church and gave Himself for her, [26] that He might sanctify and cleanse her with the washing of water by the

word, ²⁷ that He might present her to Himself a glorious church, not having spot or wrinkle or any such thing, but that she should be holy and without blemish. ²⁸ So husbands ought to love their own wives as their own bodies; he who loves his wife loves himself. ²⁹ For no one ever hated his own flesh, but nourishes and cherishes it, just as the Lord does the church. ³⁰ For we are members of His body, of His flesh and of His bones. ³¹ "For this reason a man shall leave his father and mother and be joined to his wife, and the two shall become one flesh." ³² This is a great mystery, but I speak concerning Christ and the church. ³³ Nevertheless let each one of you in particular so love his own wife as himself, and let the wife see that she respects her husband (Ephesians 5:21-33).

For the sake of this chapter on the place of love, I will like you to zoom in with me from verse twenty-five to verse twenty-nine. It says to the husbands, to love your wives "just as Christ also loved the church" that it cost him his life. This is extreme and ultimate love. This is unconditional love. It is love without limit. It is not seasonal love, which depends on the performance of one's spouse. It is undying love that knows no end. The way God wants us to love is the exact same way Christ loved the church. In other words our marriages should point to Christ. Is the church perfect? I don't think so. Is the church doing everything God wants her to do? Not in the least! With all the imperfection in the church, Christ will not give up his church for anything. If you are a true follower of Christ you cannot afford to walk away from your marriage. God expects you to continue to love your spouse, not minding whether he or she is upholding his or her commitment.

The roles and responsibilities of both the man and the woman in the marriage covenant are clearly stated in the Bible. The man's role is independent of the woman's role and vice versa. The commandment for the husbands to love their wives is independent of the commandment to the woman to submit to their own husbands. The man should not wait until the wife submits to him before he shows love to her. You have the love of God embedded in your heart. All you need to do is to express it. Remember the bible say:

He that loveth not knoweth not God; for God is love   (1 John 4:8).

God wants to manifest his love through us. We should not allow self to get in the way. Self always wants to assert itself. It does not want to be restrained in any way. It always wants to have its way. When we yield to God and choose to obey his command, by loving our spouses, self becomes helpless. The result is an outflow of the supernatural love of God through us. Glory to God! Showing love does not mean that your spouse will always make you happy. The contrary might be the case, but regardless, you choose to please God by obeying his command.

For consider him that endured such contradiction of sinners against himself, lest ye be wearied and faint in your minds (Hebrews 12:3).

Jesus went through the worst provocation any one can ever think of in the hands of the sinful man whom he came to save, but in the midst of it all he lavished his love on mankind. What they did to him was enough to make him abandon the work of redemption. Then we would have been doomed eternally. There was no sin found in him, he did nothing worthy of death, yet he willing offered himself as a sacrifice for your sins and my sins.

For scarcely for a righteous man will one die: yet peradventure for a good man some would even dare to die. But God commendeth his love toward us, in that, while we were yet sinners, Christ died for us (Romans 5:7-8).

Take a look at the book of Isaiah chapter fifty-three in verse seven,

He was oppressed, and he was afflicted, yet he opened not his mouth: he is brought as a lamb to the slaughter, and as a sheep before her shearers is dumb, so he openeth not his mouth.

Do you think the reason why he did not open his mouth was because he does not know what to say? It was love that made him not open his mouth otherwise he would have aborted the redemption work. He is love personified. That is why the scriptures enjoined us to follow his examples.

Husbands, love your wives, even as Christ also loved the church, and gave himself for it (Ephesians 5:25).

CHAPTER SEVEN

COMMUNICATION IN
MARRIAGE

I have mentioned a few things on the subject of communication in earlier chapters but because of the importance of communication in marriage I would like to devote this chapter to talk a little more on communication. Communication plays a pivotal role in marriage. Communication can make or break a marriage depending on how you treat it.

Communication is defined as the art of passing across information or feelings or thoughts to someone else, in this case your spouse. Communication is not the same as talking. Talking means to utter words but communication is to pass across information. Until one has successfully passed across his or her message, you have not communicated. It is ones responsibility to make sure who you are talking to understands what you are saying.

And even things without life giving sound, whether pipe or harp, except they give a distinction in the sounds, how shall it be known what is piped or harped? For if the trumpet gives an uncertain sound, who shall prepare himself to the battle? So likewise ye, except ye utter by the tongue words easy to be understood, how shall it be known what is spoken? for ye shall speak into the air (1 Corinthians 14:7-9).

Communication is not just passing across your feelings. What you are saying, how you are saying it, when you are saying it and how you are saying it are equally important. Wrong manners: the tone and volume of your voice is also an issue that should be taken care of in communication. You don't need to raise your voice before you make a mark.

A soft answer turneth away wrath: but grievous words stir up anger (Proverbs 15:1)

The time of anger is not the best time to talk, be wise.

He that keepeth his mouth keepeth his life: but he that openeth wide his lips shall have destruction (Proverbs 13:3).

What you say can make or break your marriage. You are going to live with the consequences of what you say.

Death and life are in the power of the tongue: and they that love it shall eat the fruit thereof (Proverbs 18:21).

Communication must be clear and complete. Make sure you are understood, don't assume that you are understood. This is because poor communication will lead to misunderstanding, and misunderstanding will lead to argument. When you argue you drive each other apart. Communication is a two way process. It involves talking and listening. Be sure to communicate with God. When you effectively communicate with God, it translates to effective communication with your spouse. Communication can be verbal or non-verbal. Good communication enhances friendship and closeness. Communication makes you open to one another. In other words it builds trust. It makes you to understand your spouse better. You have to keep the channel of communication open.

CHAPTER EIGHT

THE MARRIAGE
COVENANT

A covenant is an agreement between two parties on the basis of certain conditions. A covenant is different from a promise. A promise is a decision to do or not to do something. It can be verbal or written. One can choose not to honor his promises without any consequence. It is not so with a covenant. A covenant is made with conditions attached to it. It comes with obligations and benefits. A covenant is contractual in nature in that it is usually written, but it is always sealed, unlike ordinary contract, which may or may not be sealed. Marriage though is a legal contract between the man and the woman, but most importantly it is a covenant. In the marriage covenant it is between God who is the covenanter and both spouses who are the covenanted. It is not a covenant between the man and the woman. It is only the covenanter that can revoke the covenant. This is why divorce does not nullify the marriage. In the eyes of the Lord you are still married. That is why God calls any other marital relationship after divorce adultery (Matthew 19:9). The covenanted has no right to tamper with the covenant. The covenant of marriage is initiated by God but it is activated by the words we speak during the marriage ceremony, otherwise called the marriage vows. One of the hallmarks of a covenant is commitment. God is committed to the marriage covenant.

My covenant will I not break, nor alter the thing that is gone out of my lips (Psalm 89:34).

It takes a good understanding of the marriage covenant and the willingness to do your part to enjoy the blessings and favor that comes with the marriage relationship. This is the anchor that holds you and keeps you in your marriage against the evil storm of the enemy, which has caused many to divorce. You need to understand that God's idea of marriage is different from man's idea. To enjoy your marriage as God planned it, you must accept God's concept of marriage. The world makes fun of marriage today. They will tell you that you are trapped and that your freedom is gone. Do not believe them. In fact, the opposite is true. Marriage launches you to a dimension of liberty you have never known before. I can tell you this, marriage is good. To me, it is one of the best things that ever happened in my life. Someone would ask, "Are you married to an angel?" My answer to that is capital "NO". Angels do not marry, only the daughters of men do. All I did was to believe the word of God, the Bible, accepted his views about marriage and made the decision to live by it. I can tell you this; I am married to the best woman in the world. I have come to realize that people's opinion about you does not count when it comes to the issue of one's destiny in Christ. You should not strive to please people, only strive to please God.

When a man's ways please the Lord, he maketh even his enemies to be at peace with him (Proverbs 16:7).

Peaceful and harmonious marriage doesn't just happen. It is obedience to the terms of the covenant, everyone doing his or her part that makes it happen in a marriage relationship. God's part of the covenant is always guaranteed. It is the couples' side of the covenant that is most often compromised. That is why commitment is very important.

PRINCIPLES IN GOD'S CONCEPT OF MARRIAGE

1. LEAVE AND CLEAVE

    The man and the woman must gain parental independence. There should be no remote controlling from the parents. You must know the place that your spouse occupies. Your spouse should be number one in your priority list. There are some married people that still have their parents as their priority. This is anti- marriage covenant and has caused a lot of problems in many marriages. Thank God for our parents, for the love they invested on us, but one should be able to break away from any apron that tied one to them when one gets married. Except we let go of the old wine one cannot taste of the new wine that God has prepared for him or her.

Therefore shall a man leave his father and his mother, and shall cleave unto his wife: and they shall be one flesh (Genesis 2:24)

This does not mean that you should abandon them. That is not what I am talking about. We all have covenant obligations to your parents but they are not the priorities. It does not mean that they cannot give you advice. You must be able to make your own decisions without any parental interference. This is very important because the cleaving will not be efficient if the leaving is not complete. It is the cleaving that makes the man and his wife to be one. You must leave physically and emotionally. You must accept the responsibility for your home.

2. FAMILY STRUCTURE

In every organization there is a structure, otherwise called the chain of command. Any organization without such a structure will not be functional. For any system to run efficiently the organizational structure must be functional. When this structure is not in place there will be total disorder. The following passage of scripture sheds more light to this issue.

In those days there was no king in Israel: every man did that which was right in his own eyes (Judges 21:25).

Nothing can be truer than the truth. God is a God of order and have laid down a structure on how marriage covenant should operate. Everyone has his or her God given roles and responsibility. Anything short of this divine order and arrangement will be a clog in the wheels of the marriage. In the marriage set up God made man the head. Man was made the head not because he is smarter, God just chose to make him the head. The power to choose came from God, so it is not out of place for God to exercise that right. As the head, the man is expected to lead his family.

For the husband is the head of the wife, even as Christ is the head of the church: and he is the saviour of the body (Ephesians 5:23).

He is the spiritual head, he is the physical head, and he is the financial head. As the spiritual head, he is the priest of the family or home. He should lead his family to God in prayer, praise and worship. Many men have left this role in pursuit of the things of this world and cover over the home is removed. The home should come first before careers and jobs. No matter what you are doing in life, take care of your family. As the physical head, he should be able to take decisions in the family. He can take advice from the wife but he should take the decision. Train the children and instill discipline in them (Proverb 22:6). Live for your family, love them and die for them. As the financial head he is to provide for his family. He should cater for the welfare of his family. Your wife is the helper to help you fulfill these God given roles and responsibilities.

And the Lord God said, It is not good that the man should be alone; I will make him an help meet for him (Genesis 2:18). She is the home maker, making the home conducive for every member of the family.

3. LOVE AND SUBMISSION

Love and submission are two vital ingredients that make marriage work as God intended it to work. The duo is the tool that God employs to strip the man and the woman of selfishness. Selfishness is a major cause of crisis in homes. It will skew any one from aligning with God's best. When we successfully apply ourselves to the requirements, to love and to submit, then we can break away from the hold of selfishness.

Wives, submit yourselves unto your own husbands, as unto the Lord (Ephesians 5:22)

To submit means to bring one's self under the authority or leadership of another. Submission does not have a punitive connotation neither is it an indication of inferiority or weakness. It is simply the way God set the marriage union to work. It may not be a popular thing to do in the modern world but it is a biblical concept. Submission is the woman's part in the marriage covenant. Everyone is expected to play his or her part for the marriage covenant to work as God intended. God's part in the covenant is always guaranteed. When a woman submits to her own husband she is simply obeying God and she will receive the blessings of the Lord and the husband will honor her. She stands to gain both from God and from her husband. God expects the woman to submit to her husband in all things. When a woman is submissive, she goes the direction the husband is going. She co-operates with the husband. She does not oppose the husband's decisions, even if those decisions seem foolish. She can make her suggestions but let the man be the one to makes the decision, except he gives her the authority to decide. Submission is an attitude of the heart. It has nothing to do with your husband's perfection. Any woman that refuse to be flexible, and is not ready to change will definitely have trouble with the husband. It takes humility to submit. God will give you the grace to submit to your own husband in Jesus name.

To the man, God commands him to love his wife:

Husbands, love your wives, even as Christ also loved the church, and gave himself for it (Ephesians 5:25)

This kind of love is God's kind of love and not the world's kind of love. When a man genuinely loves his wife it becomes absolutely impossible to divorce her. Love is the tool that God used to win the world that hated him.

For God so loved the world, that he gave his only begotten Son, that whosoever believeth in him should not perish, but have everlasting life
(John 3:16).

This kind of love is sacrificial, and it does not fail. It does not look for what to get in return. You don't love her because of her cooking, her beauty or the money she makes. It a decision you make it is not an emotion you feel. You just love her unconditionally because God commanded you to. No strings attached. You don't hold back your love until she changes. You must love her continuously, even in the times she is not doing things that makes you happy. Demonstrate your love, not only by words. Give her gifts, material gifts, gift of time, and so on. God will surely reward your obedience to his commands.

CHAPTER NINE

MAKING IT RIGHT

WHAT MUST I DO: THERE IS NEED FOR REPENTANCE AND CONFESSION

This is my candid advice to anyone that might have divorced due to one reason or the other, and married another. Every violation of the commands of the scripture is sin. The bible says:

All unrighteousness is sin: and there is a sin not unto death (1 John 5:17).

The word unrighteousness connotes disobedience. It is a dangerous thing to live in sin. God will surely punish sin. The bible says that the sinner will not go unpunished, and that it is a fearful thing to fall into the hand of the living God.

Though hand join in hand, the wicked shall not be unpunished: but the seed of the righteous shall be delivered (Proverbs 11:21).

It is a fearful thing to fall into the hands of the living God (Hebrews 10:31).

Hebrews chapter two verses one to three put it this way:

Therefore we ought to give the more earnest heed to the things which we have heard, lest at any time we should let them slip. For if the word spoken by angels was stedfast, and every transgression and disobedience received a just recompence of reward; How shall we escape, if we neglect so great salvation; which at the first began to be spoken by the Lord, and was confirmed unto us by them that heard him.

One dangerous thing about the law of God that many have not grasped is the fact that the law of God is supernatural. There will be no visible or tangible evidence at the beginning as a result of its violation. Don't ever mistake that to mean that nothing has happened. You don't want to regret at the end of the day. That is why repentance is critical.

Don't be deceived, one day this life will be over and we will all stand before God, the judge of the whole earth, to give account of our lives. Given the brevity of life and the endlessness of eternity one needs to do something now so as not to jeopardize his or her future in eternity. There is need for repentance. Repentance simply means a change in direction which is as a result of a change in mind. Repentance also means to turn away from sin. It is only the Christian faith that teaches repentance. It is a word many hate to hear today. It may seem to be an old fashioned word but it is still required if one wants to make things right with God. Just feeling bad about a sinful or a bad habit will not fix it. You need to confess it before God. Confession is admitting your wrong and acknowledging that God is right. Confession must follow repentance if one desires a change.

One may ask; can I return to my former spouse after getting a divorce? You may, if you have not gone to be with another man or another woman as the case may be, in a sexual relationship. Otherwise, it is an emphatic no. When one or both parties have gone to be joined to another man or woman after a divorce, they cannot come to their previous spouse. They have done treacherously to their marriage covenant. All you can do at this point is to repent before God and ask for his forgiveness. Then you should ask for forgiveness from your former spouse. If you are a child of God and you have gone through a divorce, here is my advice for you, if you are already in a new marriage, both you and your present spouse should ask for forgiveness from your previous spouse. Whether you are the one that is responsible for the divorce or not, it does not matter. I don't claim to know it all in any way, but I have the spirit of God. All I am saying is this: You don't want to have anything that will count against you on that day, the day of judgment. I will like to put this two scriptures together in order to paint a clearer picture of what I am trying to convey to you.

And I say unto you, Whosoever shall put away his wife, except it be for fornication, and shall marry another, committeth adultery: and whoso marrieth her which is put away doth commit adultery (Matthew 19:9).

Know ye not that the unrighteous shall not inherit the kingdom of God? Be not deceived: neither fornicators, nor idolaters, nor adulterers, nor effeminate, nor abusers of themselves with mankind, Nor thieves, nor covetous, nor drunkards, nor revilers, nor extortioners, shall inherit the kingdom of God (1 Corinthians 6:9-10).

God is the one that decides who goes to heaven, not any pastor. When John the Baptist came preaching the baptism of repentance for the remission of sins in the book of Luke chapter three the people came to him to ask him what they should do.

And the people asked him, saying, What shall we do then? He answereth and saith unto them, He that hath two coats, let him impart to him that hath none; and he that hath meat, let him do likewise. Then came also publicans to be baptized, and said unto him, Master, what shall we do? And he said unto them, Exact no more than that which is appointed you. And the soldiers likewise demanded of him, saying, And what shall we do? And he said unto them, Do violence to no man, neither accuse any falsely; and be content with your wages (Luke 3:10-14).

There is what to do as a sign of genuine repentance.

Here is an example of what I am trying to communicate to you. It is an imaginary phone conversation between two ex-spouses. Oscar and Susie spent only five years in their marriage before their marriage was ended in a legal divorce. About a year after their divorce, Oscar came to the knowledge of the truth of God's word and the righteous requirements of the scriptures. He chose to make things right with his ex-wife. Here is how the phone conversation went.

Oscar: Hello Susie

Susie: Hello, who is this?

Oscar: Susie, this is Oscar.

Susie: Oscar! Which Oscar?

Oscar: your ex

Susie: yes, what can I do for you?

Oscar: do you have a few minutes to talk? There is something important I want to discuss with you.

Susie: go ahead

Oscar: Can you do me a favor; I want to ask for your forgiveness for whatever I might have done wrong to you in the course of our marriage that might have led to our divorce. I was ignorant of the righteous requirement of the Lord in marriage. Obviously, I have my mistakes but find grace in your heart to forgive me. I have repented before God but I need to make things right with you. That is why I called.

Do not go beyond this point. No argument, nothing more nothing less. If you sincerely do this from your heart God who sees in secret will surely reward you. He will not refuse a contrite heart. *The sacrifices of God are a broken spirit: a broken and a contrite heart, O God, thou wilt not despise* (Psalm 51:17). Whatever is your ex-spouse's response is not your obligation. You have played your part. Then you can move on with your life, and be determined to nurture and care for your present relationship. Learn from your past mistakes, and avoid the pitfalls.

CHAPTER TEN

REAL PEOPLE, REAL PROBLEM, AND REAL SOLUTIONS

The stories you will read in this chapter are true life stories of couples, like any other couples, that have experienced a face off or hotspot situations in their marriages, what the issue was, how they resolved it. I asked some of my colleagues at work to share their personal experiences for the purpose of this book which they obliged. One ended in a divorce and others are still committed to their marriages. My prayer for every one of them is that God will knit their hearts together with his love, and perfect all that concerns them in Jesus name. I have mentioned this earlier; there is no marriage that is immune to problem throughout the lifespan of that marriage. God did not promise any one a problem-free life, but he assured us of his deliverance from any problem we might encounter.

But now, thus says the LORD, who created you, O Jacob, And He who formed you, O Israel: "Fear not, for I have redeemed you; I have called you by your name; You are Mine. When you pass through the waters, I will be with you; And through the rivers, they shall not overflow you. When you walk through the fire, you shall not be burned, Nor shall the flame scorch you. (Isaiah 43:1-2 NKJV)

It does not matter if it is actual waters, rivers and fire, or situational ones, God promises to deliver his people. Looking at the above scripture, you will notice that there is a progression in intensity or magnitude of the situation. It went from waters (i.e floods) to rivers and from rivers to fire. On a scale of one to ten, one being the least problematic and ten, the most problematic, the fire situation should rank the highest. Fire situations are those crisis points at which both spouses are convinced that they have had enough and will like to end it all. Whichever is the case, waters, rivers or fire situations; God promises to see one through. All we need is to keep on trusting him and obeying his instructions. Those problems are just different phases in the journey of the marriage that will definitely be phased out in Jesus name. Amen!

MONEY PROBLEM

My wife and I both share a bank account. This bank account is both of our payroll checks together. My wife has always been responsible for paying the bills, because at her job she has her own computer and access to the internet to pay bills online. One day I complained that I never carry enough cash to buy something on a whim if I ever wanted. At first my wife reminded me that I have access to the bank account as well as her. My complaint was that anytime I purchased something with my debit card, she will know right away, since we have apps on our smart phones that give us alerts if our bank account was ever hacked and there was excess spending. Not that I was trying to hide something from her, but I was always questioned about what I purchased, whether it was something I really needed or just wanted. It was kind of belittling to me, in my own opinion, that I was always questioned, as if I needed permission to spend some of my own hard earned money. This became an argument every time I withdraw cash on payday. To resolve the issue, we both agreed that since she had the advantage of knowing when we have extra spending money, because she pays the bills online and always know the balance on our spending account. We both agreed that I should open a personal account and a small amount would be deposited directly out of my payroll check. That would be for gas in my truck and anything else I could afford with this small amount. We also agreed that if I ever got to the point where my spending would be out of control that I would close the account and go back to the way things were before. To this day we haven't had an argument over our finances and I occasionally surprise her with gifts, which was difficult in the past, since she always question a purchase from a pricey department store or the occasional jewelry store purchase.

MY BELIEFS VERSES HIS CHOICES

A large conflict my husband and I have had recently is my judgment of his eating schedule and what he was conning, the choices he was making.

I believe I take care of myself very well, always making sure I eat, and that I eat healthy. I understand food is the fuel of the body, and that you are what you eat. Being a busy and hardworking man, I know it is crucial for him to eat and eat healthy. But with the long hours he puts in at the office, the last thing he wants is his wife nagging him for eating "wrong", for forcing him to think if what he is about to consume is "healthy" for him. He has enough stressful decisions to make at work, having a wife who judges him for treating himself to what he wanted ("unhealthy options") was the last thing he wanted or needed. My judgment of him went on for months until one night we were at a gas station, looking for snacks and I judged him negatively about his food options. He didn't purchase the food. Instead, he took me home, dropped me off and left for a few hours to chill out. Eventually he came home. When he did, he filed me in, kindly and gently told me about how I hurt his feelings when I negatively judge him. He shared his thoughts and reasoning with me, why he had to drop me off along with why his feelings were affected when I judged him. I listened to all he has to say. He was aware it may take me a little time to stop my eye looks and judging sentences. But I told him I would work on catching myself in those moments because I respect him and our relationships. Now, I have trained myself to be aware of those moments when I could send judging signals around food choices to my husband. If I see him choosing something I don't approve or wouldn't chose myself, I smile and remember my husband had a hard long day at work and deserves to treat himself as he wishes.

YOUNG AND INEXPIRIENCED

We were young and inexperienced, and as many young marriages have issues in their marital relationships, so do we. Finances and lack of communication were the main elements that killed our marriage. Despite the troubles we were having, I wanted to make it work but she didn't. She felt she couldn't continue with the marriage, and she filed for a divorce. After our marriage was ended we discovered things about each other that weren't exposed during our marriage. Our childhood was a sad one and it played a huge role in our relationship. Personally I felt my life had no meaning any more at the time it all ended. My wife and my children were everything to me, my motive to live. There was so much pain and scars in our upbringing but we couldn't detect it at the time because we did not have Christ in our lives. Christ is our detector, our protector and our guide. He detects the enemy in any form he may appear, and then he protects us from him. Most importantly, he guides us through life with assurance of victory. How we raise our children is very important. We must instill in their minds who Christ is and that without him our lives will have no direction. It is our responsibility as parents to teach them to seek God's kingdom and to prepare them for life ahead, for his glory.

FINAL THOUGHTS

THE NEED FOR SALVATION:

RECEIVE JESUS CHRIST THROUGH FAITH

There are certain realms of relational experiences that one cannot access without salvation, both with God and other individuals, including your spouse. Even with well cultured manners, good intentions and determinations, there are still people you cannot please and it is difficult to relate with such people. This is because the human nature comes with certain limitations (sin) that make it impossible for one to live as God intended him to. For example; it is humanly impossible to be nice to someone that is nasty to you. The goal of salvation is not the forgiveness of sin rather it is restoring man's relationship with God. Forgiveness of sin is just the means to achieve that goal.

Have you been redeemed from the power of sin? Jesus came that through the forgiveness of your sin you might be reconciled to God. Do not allow the death of Jesus to be in vain in your life. He said in Matthew chapter eleven verse twenty-eight "*Come unto me all ye that labor and are heavy laden, and I will give you rest.* In John 6:37 Jesus said "*All that the father giveth me shall come to me, and him that cometh to me I will in no wise cast out". "Behold I stand at the door, and knock: if any man hear my voice and open the door, I will come in to him, and will sup with him and he with me"* (Rev.3:20).

THE THREE BASIC STEPS TO SALVATION
(ABC of Salvation)

Acknowledge your sin before God:

He that covereth his sins shall not prosper: but whoso confesseth and forsaketh them shall have mercy (Proverbs 28:13).

Believe in your heart that Jesus died and rose again on third day to justify you.

"For with the heart man believeth unto righteousness; and with the mouth confession is made unto salvation" (Romans 10:10)

Confess Jesus as your Lord and savior.

That if thou shalt confess with thy mouth the Lord Jesus, and shalt believe in thine heart that God hath raised him from the dead, thou shalt be saved (Romans 10:9).

You need to pray out these prayers and mean it in your heart.

PRAYER:

Dear Lord Jesus, I am a sinner, I believe you are the Son of God; you died for my sins and rose again on the third day to justify me. I repent of all my sins. Forgive me and wash me clean with your precious blood. Deliver me from the power of sin and of Satan. I receive you right now into my heart, and into my life to be my personal Lord and savior. Fill me with your precious Holy Spirit. I thank you dear Lord for saving my soul. I pray in Jesus name. Amen.

CONGRATULATIONS AND WELCOME INTO THE FAMILY OF GOD.

BLESS YOUR MARRIAGE DON'T CURSE IT

The words we speak are not ordinary words. They have creative power. One needs to be careful about the things one says about ones marriage. Words are seeds. What one says today will germinate tomorrow and bear fruit after its kind.

Say unto them, As truly as I live, saith the Lord, as ye have spoken in mine ears, so will I do to you (Numbers 14:28).

You need to speak life into your marriage. In other words, speak from God's perspective and speak what you desire in your marriage. Pastor John Omewah of the Redeemed Christian Church of God, Heaven's Glorious Embassy once said that to be realistic is to be negative. So do not speak according to what you see, speak according to your desire. One of the attributes of words is that they are creative. What you say is what you see.

Death and life are in the power of the tongue: and they that love it shall eat the fruit thereof (Proverbs 18:21)

Therefore I say unto you, What things so ever ye desire, when ye pray, believe that ye receive them, and ye shall have them (Mark 11:24)

I DELARE AND DECREE THAT:

My marriage shall be a blessing, it does not matter what it may look like now. God has a plan for my marriage, a plan of peace not of evil.

My marriage is changing for good to the glory of God.

I have an enviable marriage that reflects the glory of God.

My wife is the best woman in the world.

Go ahead and add to the list of what you want to see in your marriage. May the Almighty God honor your words even as you honor him in Jesus's name. Amen! And Amen!

OTHER BOOKS BY THE AUTHOR

Gospel Power Magazine

The Sex Conspiracy

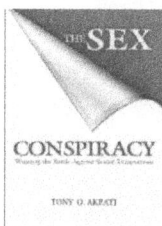

www.ingramcontent.com/pod-product-compliance
Lightning Source LLC
Chambersburg PA
CBHW060306050426
42448CB00009B/1757